*The musings of a lost college student.
For those who believe they will never be found.*

*As always, thank you for the support. it truly means the world to me.
one note before you continue, anytime you see*
{

}
That is the part where you will become the poet yourself. there is no rubric, no outline, no requirements, put whatever you feel belongs there. Bleed on the page with me. write wherever you would like. the brackets are simply suggestions. this book is now yours.

prologue

get a pen, okay?
permanent, no pencil.
it's important.

Now, I want you to write down your biggest wish.
Imagine I'm your genie.

Go ahead I'll wait…

{

}

impression of depressed shel silverstein

may the day come
when you no longer feel the need to hold your head hung
the day where the sun, and the moon rise even higher
and your gun,
you can put it down, son.

may the day never come when your fog dissipates,
for these clouds are what keep us safe.

you really think you could handle knowing what's out there?
we created this place
for a reason.
you look beaten.

may i request
that when the words stop flowing
the eyes stop glowing

we can finally rest?

people lie

at this point,
if I hear it again,
my veins will be drained of their blood,
my head will spin in reverse,
my hands will shakily release the ledge.

because people,
people fucking lie.

do what makes you happy, clear your mind, focus on yourself, exercise, eat well, try to sleep, routine, routine, routine, emotional support, comfortable living space, do what makes you happy, routine, routine, routine.

a hoax, changes nothing.
it's a lie, to give you hope that your clouds will clear,
shadows absolved by the light.

do you really know what routine means?
it means doing the same thing over and over and expecting a smile to eventually creep over your face.

do you really know what insanity means?
it means doing the same thing over and over and expecting something to change.

why, do people lie?
why?

im going insane.

forever frozen

i am grateful.

i have to be.
i'm grateful for my dog, who I'm convinced is me but in a dog's body.

i am grateful because i know I can do anything if I put in the work,
but what if I just can't work anymore?

sometimes, i am grateful for the nighttime.
the darkness creeps in, gives me a hug and disappears into the corners of the room.

sometimes, i am grateful that the people I have lost can never grow old in my mind.
forever frozen images, broken memories.
but at least there are no gray hairs. no years spent apart,
sitting by a bedside waiting for the day…

no, i am grateful.

we control our memories, the ones that stick with us until we die. the ones that spill out of the hourglass with each passing year.

so if you don't want to forget.
think about it.
tell yourself: "it is forever frozen"
for that, i am grateful.

daydream

my life used to be in color.

but, to tell you the truth,
i can't remember what that was like.

all i know is that it isn't anymore.

----

monochrome

i see your smile,
but it's gray.

i think to myself while looking in the mirror.

i see the sun,
but it's gray.

the dripping honey is nothing but puffs of ash growing larger.

every face i pass, friend or stranger, i look into their eyes.

I see nothing but gray.

magic trick

fire,
lungs fill with smoke,
my heart screams.

i pour water on the flames.

my heart screams.
i pour water on it.
my heart screams.
i pour water on it.

no matter how loud it screams my face does not flinch.
my eyes are silent.

my heart screams,
but who cares.

sewn closed

a piece of thread jumps side to side across my lips,
i put it there myself, of course.

because what is the point of talking

if no one is listening

{

}

perfect birthday

what is my perfect birthday, you ask?

a beach,
somewhere the november sun warms my heart,

somewhere safe from flashbacks of blowing out candles and a genuine smile, a genuine laugh.

somewhere the waves warm every inch of my skin.

somewhere free of people who are saved in my phone, but not in my memories.

and somewhere to play, play like i'm a kid until i feel free again.

"i would just like to be warm and safe", i say.

{

}

rant cont.

life is fucking scary.

how are people expected to work for 5/7ths of every week of their adult life. have a job, to make money, to survive, while never really getting what they want. the way we live, the standard, STOPS PEOPLE FROM BEING HAPPY.

i feel like it wasn't meant to be like this. dreams shouldn't be to make a lot of money and yet that's all we can think about when we close our eyes. i want to travel, i want to have things that make me happy, but i do not want to live every day of my damn life being unhappy, unsatisfied, other than for about 5 waking hours a day.

i want to live to work, make money so that i can adventure. but do not get it twisted, i do not want money. i do not like money. but it is the only way to happiness in my opinion. i do not want to work, don't want to contribute to this fucked up society.

there are very few people who win in this situation.
and i'm starting to realize with each passing day, our odds for being them are slipping away.

knock knock part 2

hello? who's out there?

a scraggly, torn-up shadow is what was.
sitting there, each inch surrounded by the dissipating fog.

the knocks only happen at night.
as if the sunlight prevents anyone, anything from coming near the house.
surrounded by a protective bubble of dripping yellow.

the noise against the panels of my cabin wakes me up.
clawing, scratching, tearing piece from piece. they're trying to get in.

so i get up with a smile
and open the door.

{

}

Who's there?

Dust

across the expanse of grass, sand, water, rays of sunlight
i see it floating.

a sphere bouncing across the surface of the earth.
rolling and soaring like a part of the wind

millions of little specks
piece together this dust ball
sparkling, shining,
flying from edge to edge, dropping to the bottom

all the little planets, stars, and on one special little piece

I see you.

Me and you.

the fault of the human body

if you run too hard sometimes you
might hurt your legs

if you push too hard sometimes you'll
be sore the next day

if you think too hard sometimes
your brain might hurt
your hands might shake
your eyes might spin
your heart might break

it's normal?

patience,

we spend our lives waiting,
waiting to be older,
waiting to have a dog,
or a house,
waiting for the right "love",
waiting to make a family,
waiting for the day they just might feel the same rush,

the smile and the laugh they once had.

i cant stop running

i had this thought on how to pass time
i would start counting the seconds in a day,
pay attention to nothing else,
eyes closed, simply thinking aloud to myself
1, 2, 3, 4…
the seconds turned to minutes
walking down the street
minutes to hours
reading
to days
in the midst of people but utterly alone
to weeks
running, running, running,
to months
3,144,999,998, 3,144,999,999, 3,145,000,000…

and just like that i was done,
it's too bad i missed the sunset.

the void

we look up in the sky in search of answers,
a word spelled out in the clouds,
a face of comfort,
stars creating a path for us to follow.

an escape from the pain we feel

the ever expanding space, universe, galaxy, must have the answers because
They sure as hell aren't down here.

and so we look…

and we wait…

because it's time,
For another star to enter the stage.

the scarlet rose

pacing through the garden,
i look up at the sky and ask,
"pardon, but could you tell me about this one?"

light peeks through the cracks, the clouds shift,
and the sky says, "that is life's gift,
the Scarlet Rose.

roses are everywhere you look, as beautiful as doves,
a sign of true love.

most roses wither, the color fades,
turn to different shades of gray

but look at this one,
as brightly shining as the sun, no wilts
no drops of blood slipping down the petals, flawlessly settled,

this one is different,
knows how to protect,
this Rose is
Perfect."

nothing is permanent

you know, nothing feels real until it's already passed.

time heals all wounds because we do not process events as they happen.
we literally cannot live in the moment because everything is always changing, right?

school feels never-ending, until after you graduate.
we can still see outlines of those we've lost around every corner,
my brain can't accept change as it happens.

until you.

you made me feel life again
this feels real, as it's happening, not after.
i can see the road in front of me shift, change, while you hold my hand,
i see the hourglass finish before the sand even drops,
you trace your fingers across my chest, and fuse the cracks in my heart
your smile opens my eyes,
and the curl of your lips clears the skies.

for once, for fucking once, with you:
i can feel the love, i can feel the stings,

because of you
i know my reality:

it's us.

tell me about yours:

{

}

mini me

my friend taught me this trick,
you close your eyes, all the way and tight,
and in that darkness you picture
a younger version of yourself
Standing at your feet.

you're flooded with the memories they haven't yet made,
the pain they haven't felt,
the scars, the marks, they don't have.

you wrap your arms around and squeeze yourself tight,
you make sure there's no chance of you slipping away
and you whisper in your ear,
"everything will be ok"

Even though you know it won't be.

scared of the dark

i used to be scared of the dark,
the flood of endless possibilities
of terrors
the strain of a reluctant peek into what could be

darkness can be intimidating.
but here's the thing:
im not afraid anymore,
in fact, i enjoy being surrounded by it.
the feeling of being coddled in the arms of shadows,

the darkness makes me admit that there is no world out there
nothing to be seen, nothing to be done
nowhere to run
so i lay here in bed,
straining for a reluctant peek into what could be
wishing to get out of my head.

relapse

sometimes i feel like i'm not meant for this life,
the water just a little too blue,
the edges a bit sharp
something just slightly off,

nothing feels right,
maybe it's light,
the change,
something's strange,

i think it's the shadow behind me
Whispering in my ear

Maybe these thoughts aren't yours to hear

existential

i think about dying a lot,
not in that sad way that everyone pictures
but i just simply don't know how much longer i can do this for,
this isn't a cry for help or to say that i'm lonely,
i have people, great people,
but they don't change the fact that i can't figure out what this is all for.
i can't find the meaning i used to have in my life no matter how hard i look,
i can't feel it when you touch me no matter how hard i focus

so i think about dying because at least then I might have some answers.

whisper

the thing that's fucked up about losing your parent
is that everytime you look in the mirror
you can see the whisper of their ghost.
they stare right back at you,
no matter how much you try not to see it.

they are frozen in time but
You still see them age on your own face
the eyes, the hair, the voice, the empathy,
it's always there staring right back at you.

that's why
I don't look in the mirror.

son

i kinda wanna name my son after my dog,
But wait wait wait hold on hear me out:
Bear the dog,
Baer the human.
kinda cute.

here's the other thing:
i got lucky with this dog. or maybe i'm just delusional but
i see myself in this dog. people always say we look the same
but the crazy thing is we act the same too.

we literally both take the same dosage of Prozac.

this dog was meant for me, and it was a struggle to be a
college student with a dog. and i know it's dramatic but i
became a dad and he's my best friend and I know that the
decision to get him was one of fate.

and that's the type of bond i want in my son.
what do you think?

{

}

backspace

i just want to be noticed
someone to look at me, stop me, say hey you look familiar,
hey you okay? hey...anything really.
sometimes i have to remind myself that life isn't a tv show

i ache for human contact, connection, anything besides the
same old lonesomeness.
because
i swear to god my shadow is more visible than i am

my words were erased before i wrote them.

{ }

earth

sometimes I worry about having kids
Not cause I'm worried about being a dad or
Having a family or anything like that.

but I'm worried about the state of the world,
the crumbling pieces of society,
the clear lines dividing us becoming clearer.
will there be war?

will trees be melted away, will the earth be a desert?
i don't want my children to live on a planet where
Extinction reaches more than just exotic animals
Where there are no mountains to hike,
Lakes to swim in,

I don't want my children to live on a planet
Where there isn't
Life to live.

the problem

my heart wants a deep ocean
with sharks and whales
but
I keep fishing in a puddle

{

}

feature poem by my dear friend Abigale Strader.

voices

i've been hearing this voice in my head when i sleep again,
i'd like to imagine it's you

but i'm worried it's just what i think you would sound like

{

}

late night drive

for a while, i think i got lost

the roads were blocked;
my mind tried to drive through anyway

i think the car slipped across the water?
we definitely flipped.
i don't know how we stopped,

but we're at a red light now.

wake up.

first day of summer

do you want to go for a walk?

because they put the fire out
of the sky.
they must've used a lot of tears.

wind is pretty strong today,
i'm guessing it's the racing thoughts.
there one goes now!!!

"...everythingisfallingaparteverythingisfallingapartEVERYTHINGISFALLINGAPARTTTT"

jeez.
anyway, it's still better than it was a few days ago!
look how the sun is shining, the clouds whispering to each other.

the grass is green, the water blue,
life may suck
but happiness is in you:)

meh

you have to be depressed
before you can truly *feel* happiness

the difference

im tired of wasting my time being afraid
my hands dripping with sweat
legs like freaking pogo sticks

i keep my lips straight
my eyes forward
but inside my head the fear runs rampant
inside my head
i build cities
but
the fear is quick
soon enough the buildings crumble to pieces.

so i look at myself in the mirror
my eyes forward
my lips curled

and i tell myself again
"danger is very real,
but fear is a choice"

set your heart ablaze (Demon Slayer)

i heard this quote recently.

but be quite careful
because the longer it burns
the more difficult it will be to extinguish.

unless, that is,

you never put it out.

thank you, rengoku.

i'm home

as i barge through the creaking door
toss my backpack into the corner
slip my shoes off and press my feet on the cold stone floors

i can hear music from around the corner
off-key humming, kitchenware clanging against pots,
clouds of the aroma softly suffocating me

i brace myself with a smile, a soft chuckle
as i begin to make strides towards the noise
the sun falls out of the sky

when my eyes open
i'm laying on the couch wrapped in the usual blanket

i can hear your snoring without even turning my head,
but i look anyway, if not for one last glimpse,
asleep.
i guess that means i can close my eyes too.

-im surprised i can still remember all the details.

liquid sunshine

it took a while,
but i finally caught a handful.

it's burning the hell out of my hand,
slipping through the cracks between my fingers
dripping down my forearm

but there's no way i let go
i need this
you really don't understand
how BADLY i need this.

now, hold out that jar,
we need to make sure this lasts forever.

in order to combat love,

i wish it made sense
but the fun part of this fucked up world is that
nothing has to.

you can't,
you know you can't,
and because you want to, you're losing yourself
stumbling into the shadows,
it's a black hole.

but you are tough enough to move through it.

stop making the easy choice
bruising yourself
over and over

how are you ever gonna heal?

"growth"

here's the thing
if i asked you what it means,
what it really means,
i don't think you could tell me.

i don't think anyone knows.

it changes varying on perspective,
a little can be a lot,
a lot can be a little.

with the shift of time
A step forward could turn out to be a step back,
A step back could turn out to be 10 steps forward.

Maybe this doesn't make sense.
But neither does that stupid word.

hopeful

i've been having this dream

where i wake up, feeling safe and warm
again, the way i used to.
noises flow from the lower floors of the house
trickling their way around the house. the sound reminds me

that someone is there, so long as i'm not the
only one, there is no reason to panic yet.

dream again, for
in that world, I'll never be alone
ever.

-read the 1st letter of each line

after life

sometimes i convince myself that
i'm a ghost.

trapped in a permanent state of observation,
locked in my own thoughts.
i must be
that's why no one can see me

i pace up and down the street, just to see if i can catch a
passing glance
wish i could feel the heat, but i can't stop shivering
i dissolve into a cloud of loneliness as the thought hits me
once more.

here's hoping someone can see me.

i don't think we pay attention enough

on a daily basis,
i wonder how many of the smiles,
how many of the laughs i pass are fake.

a mask hiding the devastation underneath,
on the verge of apocalypse, descending into chaos
(is that a bit dramatic?)
it's entirely possible none of them are fake,
but at the same time the opposite is true.

there are so many subconscious assumptions our brain
makes.
anyway,

occasionally,
if the light catches it just right,

i can see the glimmer of the mask resting on your face.

"life is only as meaningful as you fool yourself into thinking it is"

i've accepted it will never have as much meaning as i want it to.

there's no words written on the wall behind the right choice of door,
no family member who is going to swoop in and bring the light back into my life,
no answers to the never ending stream of questions,

and that's okay with me.

but then the question becomes,

what to do with yourself now?

scatter

i'm starting to lose my grip
because everytime i think i have found something genuinely
real,
something dependable,
i reach out to grab it
but my hand slips through,
and it escapes away into the darkness
as if someone flipped off the light.

i don't think it is ever worth chasing them
with each passing step deeper into the shadows
i can feel my skin melting,
my organs spilling out,
until i can't feel my feet anymore
and my hands...

-man plans, God laughs

fake

i tried being a writer

but i hate what i write.

{

}

broken children

there are those of us
who were taught at a very young age
how devastating the world could be.

they didn't know at the time, couldn't have,
but that trauma,
changed not only their lives, but their brain chemistry.

the worst could happen at anytime,
so we live our lives on the edge of our seats ready to spring
up and run at any moment.

we can control our emotions because nothing is as painful as
the past.

there is a palpable grayness to the world,
the color never came back.

i know i'm not the only one,

so this for the others out there.

sounds

i can hear the past
echoing in my mind

and the future
ringing in my ears.

"where do the sounds come from"

one of my tattoos makes me sad

i kinda did it to myself on purpose.

It's a reminder of what happiness should look like.

they're frozen in time, as it all falls apart, losing everything they ever had

But still forever smiling,
because they have each other.

but gosh, that makes me feel fuckin lonely.

honey

as i watch it dissolve off my spoon
into the scalding hot cup of jasmine tea,

i wonder to myself if the world could just melt awaylike that.

just a change in state of matter,
from something to nothing.

i wonder if we could forget about money,
let go of the ropes burning into our palms,
it's funny really,
the world spins and spins but all we want it to do is stop for a second.

maybe if i look deep enough into your ocean eyes
it will all just pause
all the commotion gone,
just us
moving in slow motion,

like
honey dissolving
off a spoon.

in the eyes

it's so weird to me how in the eyes of
different individuals,
i embody an entirely separate person.

in the eyes of my family,
i am and will always be a
baby boy who doesn't know very much.

in the eyes of my friends,
i'm the poet, the joker,
the climber,

in the eyes of my dog,
i am his whole world

but when i look into my own eyes,
i see nothing.

seaside

"nothing could top this view" i blurt out as the sun slices through the horizon atop the shimmering sea.

i sit there, rubbing my hands back and forth between the sand, imagining it all slipping away through my fingers.

the voice behind me stammers… "we.. we.. we got here just in time."

i let the smile creep onto my face. i should be proud. i made it all the way here.

"hey, um.." the voice trails off.
"why are you standing all the way over there, just come here", i blurt out again.

do i really have to come get you?
i whip my head around
only to find nothing but jagged rocks and an
empty expanse of sand.

answers

i wish there was a way to know,
because i'm really fucking scared,

but i'm gonna do it anyway.

{

}

water fall

i look down at the cliff below me,
water dragged by gravity down towards the river bank

and all i can imagine is falling.

the weightless feeling as all the pressure is lifted off my shoulders,
the dizziness as i close my eyes,
the fear that any moment it could all just stop,
heart pounding,
everything moving in slow motion.

it's perfect.

so i spin on my heels, take your hand
and
we jump

let your intuition take over

the world is spinning as i walk the carpet towards the stage,
my conscious brain begins spewing thought
after thought
after
thought.

shut up, i tell it.

another thought, another, another.

why does this keep happening to me?
i've done this a million times
and yet here i am
on the verge of choking

pathetic.

i close my eyes, take a deep breath,
release
fucking release already.
come on.

i breathe again, deeper, and
i mute the sound of the thoughts
and picture in front of me

an empty blue sky.

casket

at least those we've lost will never have to attend our funerals.

{

}

let's trade pt 2

im tired of wearing my heart,
can i try on yours?

my hands are wrinkled, calloused,
but yours are so soft.
my arms blackened
but my face unscathed

my mind building cities and tearing them to shreds
what's yours making?

{

}

early mornings and dew drops

hey, really,
right here, we should stop.

you see that? right over this hill, other side of the map?
this is the perfect backdrop.

silence falls over the swishes of our shoes brushing the tall grass,
the dampened foliage rubbing against my bare leg,

nothing like this has ever come to pass-
maybe i could beg?

the sun begins pushing above the horizon, crawling to the surface. the frigid spring air is rapidly replaced by a tangibly moist breeze…

i turn my gaze to the sky in search an answer
a sign,
a.. something.

and as i stand there, entranced by the reflection of the vast ocean,

SMACK.
a single drop lands on my forehead, trickles down my cheek,

we should go back.

conversation with myself (grief)

it may seem like a simple idea,
but i had never considered it before.
here's how i'll explain it:

We have no reason to be exceptional, once we've lost those
whose opinions we hold with the highest regard.

who am i fighting to impress anymore?

who do i have to make proud?

is that why people insist they're always "with us"?
still "in our hearts" ?
is it because they have to hang onto that to keep their drive?

doesn't seem like I can care much longer.
not as in a surrender but more as
a door opening
because nothing really matters
and isn't that kinda
awesome?

my grain

i think the reason i'm okay with not doing anything,
sitting back and watching a leaf fall off the tree each day,

is because when i close my eyes and think,
I can build anything.

a city, a sunset, a candy land, a horror movie, a crack in the
sky, a door handle slipping off and clattering to the floor,
a smile so familiar
a hug that I can't quite feel
a shadow on the ceiling
promises revived from the grave
dreams to …

Maybe this is why my head fucking hurts

starlight

the way the moon is shining,
reflecting off the darkened street lamps,
beaming the pavement with a needle prick of illumination,

it's been a while since i've seen something like this.

thick, contaminated air.
the man-made radiance pouring out of the town.
and yet, in spite of it all,
even the stars have finally drudged themselves out from
behind the curtain.

thanks for coming with me yet again.
such a rare vision, i figured you had to see it.

i know you won't believe me,
but things don't have to be like this.

let it light your way.

frostbite

i love being out here.
this winter wonderland.
finally some fucking peace and quiet.
i've grown used to the way the frosty air stings my face, my fingers, my toes.
it's the sensation of pain, but it doesn't feel painful anymore.
just a passing thought,
a distraction from the downpour of snowflakes,
just numb.
i've grown used to the way i'm alone out here,
stuck in the snowglobe of my own creation,
a distraction from the fucked up world,
it's all just
numb.

stuck in the attic

the faint smell of peppermint wafts up into the attic through the cracks in the floorboards.

i slowly lower to my knees, then my stomach.
i squeeze my left eye shut and hold the right side of my face up to the cracks.
i know there's probably nothing worth seeing, but what else is there to do up here.

below me i see them again.

2 shadows, 2 mugs
steam rising above all four
i don't know what i was expecting to see.

click, CLICK.

aw, fuck.

{"   "}

passage of time

the stale summer air drifts in through my bedroom window,
it's June 2021.
but as i inhale, breathing it all in, analyzing every trace scent contained within the air,
i'm transported back years.
my mind rewinds to Autumn memories from 2008-2010,
before...

i can remember the walks to soccer practice in those fall months,
the adventures around the world of my neighborhood,
the bunk bed,
the small box tv and PlayStation 2,
nights of Halloween, flashes of costumes,
the evenings spent on the couch as a family
As a family
As a family

i swear i'm not trying to be dramatic when i say i struggle to remember what that felt like.
I think that's what time does.

in the lion's den

it's claustrophobic in here, ceilings low;
                          but it goes back pretty deep.

the walls vibrate with a glow from the warmth of the fire i lit.
i imagine there would be some stone carvings,
some old writing on tablets,
but these walls are bare, the stone unharmed by both man
and the passage of time.

Are you seeing what I'm seeing yet?

my torn-up Adidases scrape softly against the cave floors, as i
make my way deeper,
    getting lower
       onto my knees.
the twigs scattered across the floor dig into my kneecaps as i
crawl
and the walls yell at me to
                  "GO BACK"
HAH.
Jokes on them.

untitled

there's gotta be more to life than this
so please, go ahead, get your pen
and prove it to me
{

}
because I'm struggling to believe it anymore.

the other side

"you're not even listening", her tone is angry but I can see the pleading in her misty eyes.

i dig my nails deeper into the sides of my thighs, close my eyes and take a deep inhale.

"I'm sorry. let me try to understand again. Can you explain one more time?"

the words pour out once again, jabbing each nerve one by one,
my brain screams 17 different responses for every criticism you throw in my face but-

im trying, im trying, you don't get it, im trying,
-but I say nothing.
im listening to the words bouncing off the walls, i am,

but, words can only explain so much,
if i get lost in your eyes,
i think maybe you'll guide me through your emotions.
Through the anger, warmth, ache, love, despair, each and every care and pain, i promise I'm here.
just take my hand and show me.

the flow of the words steadies out,
and we sit there,
allowing ourselves to get lost from our path for just a few minutes, to go and see the other side.

I & C

tap, tap, tap,
the edge of my nail bed against the cracked mug sitting in my lap

i sneak another glance into the cup and stare
Deep, deep, deep
into the swirls of
Ivory and Caramel.

for me to take a drink
could easily constitute as a tragedy

tap, tap, tap
my foot on the gas pedal
as i push my gaze above the horizon
the fluffy ivory clouds mixing into carmel sun rays

tap, tap, tap
I wonder who that could be

death parade (Death Parade)

as an arbiter it is my job
to draw out the darkness and evaluate the state of your soul.

lost in sight

sometimes, i look into my kaleidoscope of memories when i'm searching for answers.
it doesn't exactly speak back,
but i can hear phrases echoing in the back of my head.

when i asked, no, begged for the meaning of life, i could hear
"suffer, but stay firm"

in my kaleidoscope of mirrors i'd expect to see my reflection,
But it's not my face anymore,
Just one i've spent years cultivating
But i can still see the distant traces of myself
That the sun burned into the skin long before i can remember.

before i look away from the kaleidoscope,
One last thing echoes in my head
"A clementine"

What the fuck is that suppose to mean.

{

}

merry-go-round

who told you that the world stopped spinning?
because they were being facetious,
im sorry to tell you
this train
will
never stop
until something
forces it to change course,
or maybe just fuckin' blows it up.

{

}

saying good morning to the sun

somehow my body made this switch recently. it went from
sleeping between 3am-1pm to sleeping from 11pm-5am.

i don't mind this new schedule, it makes me nostalgic.
the last time i consistently woke up this early,
i was a small kid
just trying to watch cartoons on a Saturday morning

now, you may find this strange, i don't know to be honest.
but my mind chooses when i sleep, how well i sleep, what i
see in there, everything.

the best way to deal with it is to simply adapt;
ride the wave as my forearm tattoo reminds me.

and so i rise out of bed at 5am sharp,
give my dog his Prozac
open up my laptop
and turn on some cartoons.

one by one

the inside of my mind, my imagination,
when i close my eyes and teleport to that other reality
the territory around me kinda reminds me of cyberpunk.
or matrix, or mad max, orrrrr
you get the idea.

it's a freaking wasteland.

i know, i know. it's my own fault.
i haven't been taking care of it.
it's not like i didn't want to, i just,
i can't-,
it's so hard, ya know?

so i water the sand i'm standing on
hoping it sprouts grass,
and i start killing the hijackers,
one by one.

empty page

{ i stuff my toes deeper into the sand,
my head hung like i am a little kid.
the waves are washing up and luckily i have my fluffy beasts
to protect me from the foam inching closer and closer.

i can hear the soft, sweet voices drifting out from the
illuminated back door a few meters behind me.

Alright, time to go in. }

that will be the day
the day for my dream
to come true.

Your turn:

{

}

that will be the day
the day for my dream
to come true.

lost at sea

wake up.
come on, come on, COME ON,
WAKE UP.

the rampaging waves slam themselves into the side
drops shower our skin from above and
spray across the wooden planks.

you really gotta wake up now!!
strikes of light illuminate the sky provoking the waves to rage harder.
there's nowhere for us to escape to,
but i'll be damned if i'm drowning alone.

amidst the chaos around me
i somehow discern the slightest tug on my forearm,
take my eyes off the sky and look down.

the edges of your eyelids crack open,
as my entire world is enveloped in a blinding light
accompanied with a crash.

The stupidest men
…think they can't be wrong
…don't know what they don't know
…couldn't care to sneak a glance of the blooming Daylilies
{
…

…

…

…

…

…

…

}

6/14/2021
6:51 pm
maybe i'll get lucky and die in my sleep

7:10 pm
the blazing sun peeking between the trees is whispering in my ear.
can you hear it?

8:36 pm
Just fuckin do it
Life is meaningless anyway
So, we can do whatever we want
Isn't that something?

i've worried about you

i can recognize the face of someone drowning in resentment

{

}

do u know pain (Naruto)

suffering the same fate at the hands of each other
And yet believing ourselves to be in the most "pain"
is truly the most ironic part
About this cruel world

~~~

true freedom is
being rid of the fear
of pain and of death.

once those fears are thrown aside,
there is nothing the world can do
To stop us.

What's the first thing you're going to do?
{   }

don't get it

part of the reason
my head can't stop swirling
is because of all
the blatant assumptions we make
like
"God" wants us to make only "good" decisions.

substitute the universe for God
or
morally correct for good.

heart attack

{

}

it's not my place
it's not my place
it's not my place
fucking leave.

affirmations:) (to keep me going)

all this time, and you're still weak.

draw all the lines in the sand you want,
It won't matter once the waves come and wash them all away.

tragic, yet pathetic.

better off, better off, better off

go ahead, tear your skin off into ribbons
because once the pieces of you are removed
they can do nothing but disintegrate.

show and tell

can you show me what the world looks like without
depression
because i'm just dying
to know

{

}

acknowledgements

i am not ungrateful for this life i have,
i just want you to know that.
i have things easy,
but even when i scream those words in my own ear,
i still find myself scrambling to solve every non-existent issue
i face,
i sprint, head-first, into walls i put up.
i don't get why.
when i write, i feel like i'm whining in your ear.
i'm on this cliff and
i'm losing sight of where the ledge is...
my brain clearly loves to
dance on the knife's edge.

that's okay.
things will turn out fine,
for the most part,
for most of you,
because that's the way of the world.

So,

so, supposedly, i was a pretty cute kid.
the youngest of 4,
truly, the 'baby' of the family.

"when is he gonna stop being adorable"
"when is he gonna turn into a brat"
"when is he gonna…", my sisters squeaked in my parent's ears.

so, i've got a riddle for you:
what happens when you cross a 'baby' and a distorted concept of reality from watching loved ones smile, laugh, exist one moment and lay lifeless the next??

occasionally, a decent poem.
or at least that's what y'all tell me.

look at me now, sis.

before you go

hey,
before you go

can you just-

tell me a story?

{
Tell me a story about a princess and a beanstalk

Tell me about a knight who can't slay the dragon in time

Tell me a story about a ruthless heartless villain who falls in love

I want to hear about how unicorns can fly and how kissing strangers doesn't give you herpes

Is the apple poisonous? I'm so invested in every plot twist you write.

But please please don't end with a Happily Ever After. In fact don't end at all

Tell me a story, let me lose myself in the words you speak. Keep whispering stories into my ear and don't ever stop.

-feature poem from my dear friend Nora Taplin.
}

Your Turn:
hey,
before you go

can you just-

tell me a story?

{

}

I don't want to be myself

i can't decide if life's about embracing what you are
Or trying to be something you are not.

{

}

genie again (MHA)

it is through my actions that I will realize my ultimate dream:

{

}

focus

it's what we do, we pay attention.
even when people think we're not,
when our eyes are pointed in the other direction,
our lips tied at the edges,
body closed off,
we pay attention.
what's the point otherwise?
i have to notice everything going on
I refuse to miss a single thing
that's how people get hurt

even if you're not,
I'm paying attention.

July 25th, 2021, 3:37am

okay, so like i'm depressed right
so i've been thinking about the point of it all,
and i came to the realization that my parents
literally gave their whole lives to bring their children
into this world.
wow, i guess i'm grateful lol.
and worked until they died, mentally and physically. so what am I stressing about? am I just suppose to jump into the same trap they did? give my life for some kids I don't know yet? or am I suppose to take all this blood money and do something with it? or like...
What the fuck.
is it just whatever suits me? whatever i want? that's too much to choose. i don't know.
if i wasn't blessed with each one of my ancestor's hard work and luck, i wouldn't even have the choice. that's part of the reason i get tired of it all, because this is such a great life, it's like i don't deserve it. i know i do, i know that's dramatic, but even if i do, why should i?
For what?
For who?

anxiety in the past tense

if we take the past as an example,
it's clear that
evolution only comes to those who seek out change.

so why am i so afraid of things changing?
i used to love it.
when did i lose my grip on the excitement for life?
i want to adventure,
but leaving the house drains me until im empty
i want to travel,
but the idea of leaving this city, this country, this continent,
it all seems like more effort than it's worth
not to mention how i convince myself that any one of 1
million problems will occur.

but
once i'm back home,
unpacked,
settled into my bed,
i don't regret anything.

because you can't have anxiety about the past
it's already over.

intro()

when i write i close my eyes,
squeeze them tight till it's fuzzy darkness and static stars
and i let movies play out.
frame by frame, i describe what i see around me
in this sandbox and
i just let it unfold.

or if i'm using this keyboard as an escape from the world,
i take whichever emotion has the strongest grip on my limbs
and i isolate it.
Take every sensation inflicted by it.
let it write for me and then
rip it to pieces.

You ready?

movie
{

}

let it burn
{

}

last words

if ignorance is bliss, may you never know the meaning of peace.

did i do a good job?

i never wanted to be the villain of anyone else's story, if only you could read about mine.

flashes my most charming smile
do i look afraid to you???

{

}

baggage

you know,
if you scooch your hand over
i can help you lift all that weight.

it looks pretty damn heavy,
but we're all here for you,
so open up some space
let us all

lend a hand.

----

strangers

sometimes ill be sitting, laying, staring,
and there, in the corner of the room, two eyes.

i look over, but it's nothing.
i look back, and feel the eyes staring again.

i can hear them whispering:
open up some space in your heart,
let us all,
lend a hand.

{   }

{

}

i'm so tired of being unseen, unheard, invisible,
and Fuck You for telling me to speak.

JustYou

not feeling alone is always temporary.

don't get it confused
when you walk up those stairs,
climb under those cold sheets,

when you pull up this driveway,
turn the keys & take a breath,

Who's sleeping next to you?
Who's in the passenger seat?
No one.
it's just you,
maybe some days it's not,
but we both know
it's just you.

Fuck that sucks.

but we both know that,
So at least we're together in something :)

The Winter Saga

packing snow

my sister and i made this igloo,
mm i should say she made it, i hardly did anything,
i don't really remember where we lived,
or what year it was
but i remember the igloo.

it was pretty sick.
the only downside was it was so small on the inside that only
one of us could fit in at once,
she obviously got to go first cause she built it,
but eventually my time came

i dropped to my hands and knees and crawled deep into the frigid darkness. i remember specifically thinking that i didn't want to be in there alone. but alas, i made my way in and peeked my chubby little head out the entrance so the prickly wind could kiss my cheek.

The Winter Saga

imagine the snow

the lights,
the sounds,
the people,
imagine it all,
now go:
{

}

The Winter Saga
my favorite coffee shop

this time, i do remember the year.
November, December 2017
January, February, Ma- 2018,

i only put one airpod in while filling out my college
applications because the bustling noisiness of Peet's Coffee
was so soothing.

in the evening, the fireplace warmth vibrating from the shop
wards off the polar vortex outside.

in spite of there being no fireplace lit.

i didn't even mind the soft Christmas music they were playing
mixing with my own, slightly less soft, Christmas music in
between my ears.
it was perfect.
i swear i could do anything while sitting in that coffee shop.
solve any problem.
somewhere i could be alone but
surrounded by strangers who were friends, teachers, strangers

but now,
i'm only there in my dreams.

The Winter Saga
resolution

it's not like either of us could ever run out of things to write about.

the thoughts will never stop flowing,
there will always be something new,
so that's why i'm here for you,

i want *you*
to tell me about it.

Dusk in Winter

Thank you for purchasing this book and making it to this point. I hope you found whatever it was you were looking for.

I couldn't have written this book without inspiration from the friends and world around me, so don't forget to lift your chin up and open your eyes periodically.

Presently, there is a lot of change in my life and I wrote this in search of finding a clear path for myself, if that makes sense. I didn't find all the answers, but I think I've got some. It took months and months of work and I didn't even reach the goal I was striving for...

but meh that's okay,
at least i've had something to do.

(Some blank pages are to follow for your creative enjoyment.)

until next time,
Rajan
8/4/2021, 8:11AM